Images
From My Soul

Leslie E. Stern

Illustrations by Pam Kalista

TotalRecall Publications, Inc.
www.totalrecallpress.com

TotalRecall Publications, Inc.
1103 Middlecreek

Friendswood, Texas 77546
281-992-3131   281-482-5390 Fax
www.totalrecallpress.com

All rights reserved. Except as permitted under the United States Copyright Act of 1976, No part of this publication may be reproduced, stored in a retrieval system, or transmitted in any form or by any means electronic or mechanical or by photocopying, recording, or otherwise without prior permission of the publisher. Exclusive worldwide content publication / distribution by TotalRecall Publications, Inc.

Copyright © 2012 by: Leslie E. Stern
All rights reserved

ISBN 978-1-59095-654-0
UPC # 6-43977-46540-5

Printed in the United States of America with simultaneous printings in Australia, Canada, and United Kingdom.

FIRST EDITION
1   2   3   4   5   6   7   8   9   10

The scanning, uploading and distribution of this book via the Internet or via any other means without the permission of the publisher is illegal and punishable by law. Please purchase only authorized electronic editions, and do not participate in or encourage electronic piracy of copyrighted materials. Your support of the author's rights is appreciated.

*To Pam Kalista for her artwork
that brought my spirit to life.
My love, respect, and admiration
make Pam yet another Image from my Soul.*

*Special thanks to all the Facebook,
LinkedIn, and virtual friends
who have supported my work
from the beginning.*

Table of Contents

Images Of Life

Destiny	1
Self	2
Objective Reality	4
The Real World	6
Feeling the Music	8
Poetry	10
Present Passed	12
The Beauty of Life	14
Fantasy	15
The Creative Spirit	16
The Jazz Club	18
Art	19
Virtue is Next to Godliness	20

Images of Mankind

Physical Beauty	23
A Gentleman	24
Adulthood	26
Continuity	28
O'Hara's	30
Loneliness	31
Envy	32
Football	34
Maturity	36
The Drinking Establishment	38
The Crazy World	40
The Miracle of Food	41

Images of Love

Lost Love	43
Love	44
Men are Like a Box of Chocolates	46
Mr. Right	48

Mutual Attraction	49
My Prayer for a Man	50
The Argument	52
The Eyes of a Stranger	54
The Gift of Marriage	56
The Stranger	58
The Carnal Question	61
Thief of Hearts	62
Young Love	64
Marriage Vows	67

Images of Nature

A Star's Gaze	69
Flight	70
The Sounds of Beauty	72
The Gift	74
The Beauty of Life	76
The White Rose	77
Man's Best Friend	78
The Carnal Question	79

Images of the Sea

Wealth at Sea	81
Dreams at Sea	82
The Heart of Sailing	84
Seaside Sunrise	86
A Foggy Flight	88
Life's Sail	90
The Sounds of Sailing	92
Summer Sailing	94

Images of Family

For My Mom	97
For My Fabulous Mother	98
My Godmother	100
Father of My Soul	102
Happy 70th Birthday to my Father	104
For my Late Tasha	105

Images Of Life

Destiny

That which
is written
in the stars;
that which
is pre-determined
by the strength
of nature;
that which
we call destiny.

We aspire
to the belief
because it preserves
the fantasy
that there is a plan.
That which is
due us
will surely
happen.

We question it
as though
it really exists.
We curse it
because
it does not
exist.

Self

The most difficult
person to understand,
to appreciate,
and to respect,
is our
Self.
It is the person
with whom
we are most intimate,
yet it is the person
we are most frightened
to see.

When we meet
strangers,
we may quickly understand them,
appreciate them,
or respect them.
But if we don't,
we can quickly
walk away
from them.
This we cannot do
with our
Self.

Those attributes
about our Self
That vex us
or others,
we must either
seek to change --
a most arduous task;
seek to accept --
a most depressing task;
or seek to blind our Self to its presence --
a most unproductive task.

If we do not strive
to understand our
Self,
appreciate our Self,
respect our Self,
and most importantly,
better our Self
so that we may some day
love our Self,
Life has been
a wasteful
Gift.

Objective Reality

Objective Reality
is that which we
cannot see
but must see.
It is what is right
before our eyes;
yet our eyes blind us
to its existence.
It has the limits
of our imagination;
yet our imagination
is its limitation.

Objective Reality
is that which we
dare not see
but must fight to see.
It is the beauty before us;
the pain inside us;
the love within us;
the rage among us.

Objective Reality
is the sight that will bring
these forces together
to become a soul
with complete
peace.

Without the acknowledgement
that reality is objective
we have only
rationalization;
It is that
rationalization
that keeps us blind,
and strips us
of our
hope.

The Real World

The gentle movement
of the sea;
the lilting melody
of the goldfinch;
the affectionate love
of a hug –
this beauty
is the
Real World.

The vicious
anger of drivers;
the harsh discords
of the boss;
the cruel insensitivity
of many
who surround us,
lead us to the
misconception
that this is the
Real World.

The quiet warmth
that penetrates
our soul
cannot be taken
for granted.
Viciousness can be replaced with
Love;

Harshness can be replaced with
Gentility;
It is sometimes
difficult to find,
but it is worth
the search –
for this is the
Real World.

Feeling the Music

When sounds
of melody
gently enter
your soul,
it is called
Music.
It takes
the beauty
and sensitivity
of the spirit
and raises them
to a higher
level.

Music takes
mundane conversation
and creates
an atmosphere
of pleasure
that can help
expression
find an
outlet.

But when the sounds
of melody
echo madly
within your head
so that beauty
cannot enter
your soul
and only
the pounding
of rhythm
vibrate your spirit,
it is no longer
Music –
It is merely
Noise.

Poetry

The sounds,
the tastes,
and the feelings
of poetry
emerge from the depths
of one's soul;
from the inner spirit
that can only exist
in theory –
that is why
it can never
be duplicated.

There is no lesson
to teach a soul to feel,
a spirit to soar,
or the inner freedom
to proclaim it.

There is no lesson
to teach the fingers
to place letters
in such an order
as to become
Poetry.

Poetry emerges
from a fertile mind,
an open heart,
and the need
to express
them.

Present Passed

As I sat in the cool Autumn air
amid the white wicker
and hardwood floors
of the quaint Bed & Breakfast,
I found it most difficult
to transport myself
back to the era
that endeavored to beckon me
from within its Victorian walls.

Though the homes were lovely,
the atmosphere cried out in despair:
We are living in the present -
We will sell you objects
from the past -
but we will not allow you
to enter into
its sacred spirit.

Even the drawing room
which echoed the past
by re-creating the world
it once was,
did not succeed.

It only served to tease
by displaying the surface glimpses
of days passed
without approaching
the soul
it cried to portray.
The earnest heart
of warmth and innocence
was lost.

The Beauty of Life

Is life the beauty before us?
The blue sky above
the turquoise water below;
and the shade trees that surround us?

Is life the love
we cherish internally?
The empathy that touches our soul;
the affection that surrounds us?

Or is life the anger before us?
The cynicism that tears at our soul;
the hatred that surrounds us?

Life is what we choose internally.
The beauty we choose to touch our soul;
the empathy we choose to feel;
the love we choose to surround us.

Fantasy

What are we willing
to suffer
to fulfill
a fantasy?
The pain
of excessive noise;
the exhaustion
of sleepless nights;
the claustrophobia
of crowds of strangers;
the embarrassment
of being a part of the herd.
All to witness
a fantasy
become a reality.

If we don't have good fantasies,
we have nightmares;
but fantasies
are always disappointing.
They usually
succumb
to expectations
that are too high.

The Creative Spirit

The spirit that is imbued
in the human mind to create art
is tapped by few;
only those who are able.
Others may possess
the ability to appreciate
the beauty that surrounds them
but they cannot understand
the innate ability to see life
through the eyes of potential art;
the depth,
the inner grace,
or the imagination
to transform that world into
the words of a poem,
the strokes of a painting,
or the notes of a symphony.

Those with such spirit
are able to see life
through the three-dimensional eyes
of artistic potential,
even as a child.
The intense color,
bouquet,
and form;
as though developing the sensitivity
to transform a simple flower
into a poem

while still in infant stage.
As a mere infant,
they begin to see the world around them
with a purpose;
with the inner knowledge
that one day they will be called upon
to describe that world with the eloquence
of the written word
or the fine strokes of a brush.

Most people do not even possess the ability
to detect artistic spirit;
some cannot even appreciate
the beauty and grace that surrounds them
in their daily life.
But there have always been
those members of true humanity
who were favored with the perceptive capacity
to at least appreciate the spirit in others.
They may not have been endowed with this spirit
    themselves,
but they have sensitivity
and clarity
to recognize it in those who do.
These are the patrons
that have enabled art to flourish;
without them,
the artistic spirit would simply eat away at the soul,
with no purpose
and no escape.

The Jazz Club

As I gazed
at the brick walls,
the remnants
of sweet sound
echoes the rhythmic
beauty
of moments passed.
The basses
and trebles
soothingly radiated
from the
glowing lights,
as though the music
that had just
entered my senses
was a living,
breathing,
Entity;
Its beauty permeating
all that it
had
Touched.
The remnants
of such sweet
beauty
will remain in my heart –
breathing its Life
into my
Soul.

Art

Art is the magic
of the
Spirit;
Whether it is
with
Colour,
with
Sound;
or with
Words.

Art is the essence
of Man's ability
to capture the love
within him,
the beauty around him,
and the creativity
that compels him
to translate it
for the rest
of the
World.

Virtue is Next to Godliness

Cleanliness is next to godliness?
Wash your hands
and go
to heaven?

Make your bed
and greatness
is yours?
shower daily
and no human
can surpass
you?

The creator of this parable
must not have lived
when gods walked
the earth.

Did Mohammed
smell as sweet
as a showered
Jack the Ripper?
Did Jesus' robes
rival the freshly
laundered shirt
of Adolf Hitler?

Did Buddha's breath
smell as sweet
as that of
Ted Bundy?

Cleanliness
may smell sweet
but moral character,
empathy for
one's fellow man,
the ability to love,
or creative genius –
these virtues
are far closer
to godliness
than superficial
cleanliness.

Images of Mankind

Physical Beauty

Is beauty found
in the perfection of
features?
A perfect nose?
A perfect smile?
Or is it
the lack
of perfection
that emits
true beauty?
Soft eyes -
Crooked smile -
that glow
from within.
Here lies
the deepest
and truest
of beauty -
A beauty
that can be felt
rather than
seen.

A Gentleman

It is a sad commentary
on our society
that man
who is filled
with kindness,
blessed
with consideration for others,
cursed
with inner shyness,
and dedicated
to display such respect
is labeled a homosexual.

In 1900
such a man
would be considered
a gentleman
and well received
by society.
He would be pursued
by women
for matrimony,
and pursued
by men
for friendship.

One hundred years later,
such a fine man
is considered
a freak.
I hope society
learns a lesson
from it's most gracious
past.

Adulthood

With the emergence
of adulthood
Life no longer
holds
the simplicity of youth;
the curiosity -
the immortality -
the security.
Adulthood
brings with it
the fear
and apprehension
of self-reliance;
of necessity.

With the excitement
of youth
Life holds
the unknown future;
With the perspective
of adulthood
Life holds the
reality of
potential failure.

Blindness
Kindness
Sensitivity
Love –
Where have
they gone?

Cynicism,
Bitterness,
and Hostility
are Man's new armor
that protect him
from the
Beauty
and Goodness
in the world.

Man closes his eyes
in the hope
that he will see
only Goodness;
but the Blindness
also erases the
Beauty.

Continuity

When days
become monotonous
and everything feels
like it's been done
a hundred times before,
that is the time
for reflection.

What am I doing?
Where am I going?
Who am I?
Cease feeling average.
That is the time
to take hold
of the continuity
and overcome
a difficult obstacle.

It is by
meeting a challenge
that the dreadful
continuity will cease.

Life is changing;
things are happening.
And continuity
can only continue
if the mind
is clear,
the heart
is open,
and challenges
are met.

O'Hara's

As I gazed
at the walls
the remnants of
sweet sound
echoed
the rhythmic beauty
of moments passed.
It soothingly dripped
from the glowing lights,
as though the music
was a living,
breathing
entity;
Its beauty
permeating
all
that it
had touched.

Loneliness

Being alone
is a great relief
that can turn into
loneliness
with the blink
of an eye.

Man strives
for the peace
and tranquility
of solitude
but it is only
a temporary respite
from the fear
and rejection
of society.

Envy

Why is it
that regardless of quality,
regardless of beauty,
size is what
impresses --
especially
men?

Sitting in a beautiful
outdoor cafe,
a boat slowly
glides by.
If it is the
finest sailboat built
but is only
forty feet long
no one notices.

But a large
motor yacht
struts by,
and all
of the men
react.

The women
scarcely notice.
but the men --
all of the men --
their heads turn
to catch
a glimpse.
The larger
the yacht,
the more
the attention.

The envy
of men
for something large
seems to follow
them;
at the very least,
Subconsciously.

Football

On a neutral field
they arrive;
the modern
gladiators
with only the weapons
of Wit,
of Strength,
and of
Heart.

They plunge headlong
into the bulk
before them,
trying to retain
their dignity
as they silently
weep from the pain –
hoping the spectators
see only their graceful
spirit.

They arrive full of Hate,
Anger,
and Strength.
But are they teams?
Or are they men
who want only
to survive long enough
to give
the spectators
just one more
Show?

Maturity

He sits alone;
afraid.
His heart is filled
with goodness;
with love.
But his mind
is afraid
to commit.

His soul holds the masculinity
of his years,
but his min
refuses to accept
the beauty
and the stability
of Maturity.
His fear
is not of reality
but of the demons
he believes exist
with Maturity.

The true beauty
in his life
will only begin
when fear disappears,
and it is replaced
with the acceptance
of a calm
that will fill
his soul
when he accepts
the grace
and beauty
of Adulthood.

The Drinking Establishment

Sitting at a bar
watching the people
ordering Escapism
by the glassful;
drugs to dull
their minds,
elevate their
voices,
and deaden
their ability
to be kind.
Their only hope
is that they will not remember
the humiliation
of their actions
the following
day.

Escapism;
Irresponsibility;
and Repugnance –
these are the
course of fare
at a bar.

Valuable inhibition
which was created
to maintain our sense
of Propriety,
Decency,
and Kindness
toward our fellow Man
are slowly
lost.

The Crazy World

They who create friendship
out of convenience;
They who pursue,
yet fear
attainment of the
pursuit;
They who love,
yet their soul
is empty;
They who smile,
yet their heart is
cold;
They who attend,
yet are unable
to commit;
They who speak;
yet no words
appear;
They who hear;
yet cannot
listen.

Life is filled
with
They whom
I dare not
Know.

The Miracle of Food

A delicate aroma -
The curiosity
of texture;
of sudden crunch
after a blend
of softness.
Sweetness,
Saltiness,
Tartness,
and ultimately
physical
satisfaction.

Images of Love

Lost Love

As the tears
gently glide
down my puffy cheeks,
my heart mourns
the loss of
Love.

My mind sees
the Truth;
that there was
no loss.
The love I felt
was only
Imaginary.

As the tears
begin to subside,
my broken heart
mourns
only the loss of
Mythical Love.

Love

I have spent
my entire life
trying to understand
Love
and its meaning.
Is it that which is
Given?
Or that which is
Received?

Many people
in my life
have used the words
I love you
but the meaning
has been
Empty.

When the words
I love you
emanate from
the Heart,
the Mind,
and the Actions;
When the words reflect
Selflessness,
Respect,
and the ability
to Demonstrate those
Feelings;
Then,
and only then,
will Love
be understood;
Then,
and only then,
will Love be
as rich
for the Giver
as for the Receiver;
Then,
and only then,
will the words
I love you
have meaning.

Men are Like a Box of Chocolates

Men are like
a box of chocolates;
their outer shell
is sweet
and tempting
to the palate
but the inner filling
is a total
Mystery.

If a woman
can ever
emotionally penetrate
the sweet shell;
a sweet shell
that has sometimes
been frozen
to a hard,
impenetrable,
wall of stone,
she has found
only a
Mystery.
The Mystery
of the inner workings
of the male
Soul.

She may find
the outer chocolate
that tempted her
is even more
richly supported
by the sweetness
of a caramel-filled
Heart.

But she may also find
that the illusion
of sweetness
is merely
the artificial coating
of what is really
the bitterness
of lemon peels
or the hardness
of almonds.

Mr. Right

He sneaks
into your life
without warning,
without a sound.
But he touches
your heart
with kindness,
with compassion,
and with
the warm laughter
that eases pain.

He cannot
be forced
into your life
with determination,
or with desperation.
He must appear
as if from the heavens
to soothe your loneliness;
to warm your soul.

When he appears,
his very presence
will touch your mind
with imagination,
your body
with sensuality,
and your soul
with joy.

Mutual Attraction

Sitting alone
at a table -
waiting to see
the sparkle
in a man's eye
that attracts
us to one
another.
Like a
bright star,
drawing us
toward one
another.
A binary star;
our mutual
attraction
engulfing us
in each other's
gravitation
pull.

My Prayer for a Man

May his heart
be filled
with the
love of beauty,
artistic expression,
and without
the limitations of
Mankind.

May his mind
be filled with
the spirit of Humor,
the art of Curiosity,
and
the depth of Infinite Reason.

May his soul
be filled with
the ability to
care for others,
the value of life,
the morality of centuries passed,
and the passion
that proves
Infinite Love.

May his face
be kind,
his eyes
be the window to his soul,
and his stature
provide
Infinite Security.

The Argument

A perfect teardrop
rolled down
my puffy cheek,
trickled down
my reddened nose,
and seeped into
my broken heart.
My heart cried out –
My eyes cried out –
for Love.

The voices
were so loud,
they bellowed
and roared –
until only loneliness
filled my heart.
My voice cried out –
His voice cried out –
in hatred.

Then the
frightening silence
began –
what would be
the result?
My heart cried out –
My eyes cried out –
for an answer.

He reached his
outstretched arms
to me.
They held me
oh so tight.
His eyes cried out –
His arms cried out –
with love.

The Eyes of a Stranger

My concentration
grew dim;
My mind told me
to concentrate
on the textbook.
but my heart
was fixated
upon the eyes
of a Stranger.

As he studied
the history lesson
He was unknowingly
being studied by
Me.

The eyes of
The Stranger
were deep brown;
Sensitive –
Kind –
Sincere –
They danced.

As I feigned concentration,
I wondered if
I would ever look
deeply into
those eyes
and find that they were
mirrors
to an equally beautiful
Soul.

The Gift of Marriage

Love sneaks into your life
without warning,
without a sound.
But it touches your hearts
with kindness,
with compassion,
and with the warm laughter
that eases pain.

It cannot be forced
into your life
with determination,
or with desperation.
It must appear
as if from the heavens
to soothe your
loneliness;
to warm your
soul.

When it appears,
its very presence
will touch your minds
with imagination,
and your souls
with joy.
May this Love remain
with you both
all the days
and nights
of your
lives.

The Stranger

Her black eyelashes flutter
to a quiet stop.
A slight smile
curves her lips
and the beauty
of imagination
fills her Soul.

She is sitting quietly
on a veranda,
sipping a cool lemonade
on a warm
summer evening.
the ceiling fan
whispers a subtle hum,
as it circles above
her soft, bare shoulders.

As she gazes
at the first stars
appearing through
the darkening sky,
a figure appears
from behind
the fragrant rose bushes.

Standing tall and lean,
The striking young man
presents a bouquet
of colourful wildflowers
to the started young women.
Her gaze turns
to his sensitive,
turquoise eyes
as she accepts
the gift from the outstretched arms
of The Stranger.

The Stranger
begins to speak.
The warmth of his smile
melts away any fear
from her heart.
His conversation
takes her by surprise;
his beauty does not stop
at his perfectly appointed features –
it extends throughout
his body
and his Spirit.
His soft eyes become
the window to his
Soul.

The stars
are now fading
into the magnificent
red and gold of sunrise
as The Stranger
turns to leave.

The young woman's
eyelashes flutter open.
A deep sigh
overtakes her.
She is still in the college library,
staring at
a blank sheet of paper.

The Carnal Question

She leaned
demurely
against the bar;
her long legs
void of cover,
tanned
to a golden brown.
Her breasts
were pressed tightly
against her shear,
white blouse.

As she walked
toward the exit
with all male eyes
following each stride,
she wondered
why men
only seek
carnal pleasure
with her.

Thief of Hearts

Hiding behind
the laughter
and the Cheshire Cat grins,
lies a heart
made of gold.
Though he tries to
feign toughness
and an
impenetrable heart,
his soul
always emerges
with the kindness,
sensitivity,
and general sensuality
that could steal
the heart
of any woman.

His kindness
and inner beauty
cannot hide
beneath the outer shell
that is only
a superficial wall
to protect himself
from the soul
he fears
will emerge.

But it is that soul
that has stolen
the heart
of this
Woman.

Young Love

She sat pensively
in the third row of her English class.
The teacher,
glancing in her direction,
assumed she was concentrating
on his fascinating lecture
about Romeo & Juliet
and the true meaning
of Shakespearean tragedy.
In truth,
she was daydreaming
about a handsome young man
who was quietly sitting
in the first row.

He was everything she could want;
he was handsome,
funny,
a straight-A student,
and captain of the football team.
She longingly dreamed
of his warm, hazel eyes
gazing into hers;
his lips touching hers;
his arms in a loving embrace
around her.

Periodically, he would turn
in her direction
and acknowledge her presence
but he did little more.
They spoke briefly
about the mundane subjects
that high school students embrace;
music
or homework
or the weekend's activities
but he never pursued her
as her fantasy displayed.
She did everything
within her feminine wiles
to win his love
but always to no avail.

She cried about him at night
and smiled sweetly
at him during the day.

Her girlfriends continually told her
to give up
but she could not;
she was in love with this boy
and there was little she could do
but feel the pain of his constant rejection.

One day,
he asked to speak with her
in private
after school.
Her young heart leapt;
maybe he was finally going to
pronounce his love.
All day
she fantasized;
driving her to distraction.

Finally it came;
the time for them
to meet.
His palms were damp,
his hands shook.
His feelings were to be
verbalized at last.
Her palms were damp,
her hands shook.
She silently prayed.
But his words
were an end,
not a beginning.
He was leaving town
and her reality
forever.
Such is young

Marriage Vows

Their open hearts overflow
and spill onto each person
with whom they come in contact.
Their generosity of spirit
is the most contagious disease
in the world and
those around them
are honored to have been
infected by it.
Their respect for each other
is evident in their every
word
and gesture.
The wealthiest people
on earth
are those who can call themselves
friend
or family
to these two special people.
Their deep regard for
each other
and the beauty of nature
that surrounds us
in this glorious paradise
where they chose to take their
marriage vows
will live within all of us
forever.

Images of Nature

A Star's Gaze

Sitting
amid the crowd
I gazed peacefully
skyward.
A single,
twinkling start
illuminated
the darkness.

Its strength
quietly overwhelmed
the sights
and sounds
inundating the bustling
around the
outdoor café.
No one noticed
the star's
gentle,
watchful
eyes.

Flight

The crimson bird
is larger than life --
though her size is tiny;
She creates love
through her song --
without the knowledge
of her existence.
She sings freely;
flies effortlessly;
and gives of her tune
without constraints.
She knows no other way
to express herself
but through
the beauty of her melodies.

Need humanity
be so different?
Must we be dependent
upon erroneous youthful perceptions
to guide us into the fear
that causes our tune
to be stifled;
our flight to be strained;
and our song
to be full of hate?

We, too, must
sing freely;
fly effortlessly;
and allow the world
to hear the beauty
of our melodies.

The Sounds of Beauty

Underneath the clattering
of automobiles,
Beneath the hum
of humanity,
lies a quiet beauty
that is seldom
heard.
It is the sound
of nature
that calls
to each of us.

The sweet song
of the goldfinch;
the subtle breeze
that awakens
the leaves on the trees;
the gentle splashing
of the ocean
against the shoreline
or against the hull
of a sailboat.

These are the true sounds
of Life.
They always exist –
but it is within
the mind of Man,
and within
the soul of Man
to cherish the ability
to listen
and to truly hear
the miraculous sounds
of Beauty.

The Gift

A fragile flower
in all its
simplicity.
Soft,
Fragrant,
Delicate,
Alive.

The warmth
and gentility
of its soul
have blossomed
from the sunshine,
absorbed through its
petals
an the dew
absorbed through the
Earth.

It is a gift
of Life;
A gift
of perfection;
A gift
from the heart.
A gift
that can never
be surpassed
by a gift
of superficiality
from the pocket.

The Beauty of Life

Is life
the beauty before us;
the blue sky above;
the turquoise water above;
and the shade trees surrounding us?

Is life
the love we cherish internally;
the empathy that touches our soul;
the warmth that surrounds us?

Or is life
the anger before us;
the cynicism that tears at our soul;
the hatred that surrounds us?

Life is
what our soul chooses
it to be.
The Beauty we choose
to touch our soul;
The empathy we choose
to touch our heart;
the love we choose
to touch
all that surrounds
Us.

The White Rose

There grows
a clean,
white
rose
a droplet
of dew
delicately rests
on its fragile
petal.
It's beauty
and fragrance
are
intoxicating.

Until someone
cuts it
from its root
and tries
to make it
more beautiful
by painting it
a brilliant golden.
Thus killing
its beauty
it's fragrance
and its
life.

Man's Best Friend

The heart of a dog
was conceived
by its Creator
with total freedom
to love.

It does not possess
the pain,
the anger,
or the despair
of a human heart.
It know only
how to show
Affection,
Contentment,
and provide Protection
for the recipient
of its abundant
Heart.

If only Man
could borrow
some of that love
from his Best Friend.
Then he, too,
would be
Free.

The Carnal Question

She leaned
demurely
against the bar;
her long legs
void of cover,
tanned
to a golden brown.
Her breasts
were pressed tightly
against her shear,
white blouse.

As she walked
toward the exit
with all male eyes
following each stride,
she wondered
why men
only seek
carnal pleasure
from her
and not love.

Images of the Sea

Wealth at Sea

Regardless of any turmoil on land
the gentle breeze
and calm waves at sea
can transform it all
into perfect tranquility.

The sound of the waves,
the scent of saltwater,
and the endless blue
of the sky above
and the sea below
erase all tension
from our spirit.

Kindness
replaces hostility;
Laughter
replaces tears;
Cognizance
replaces fear.
At sea
there are no superficial signs
of wealth;
there are only
the manifestations
of wealth
found within each of us,
which is truly
the only wealth
we possess.

Dreams at Sea

There is no Beauty
like a full moon at Sea.
A calm breeze,
The gentle movement.
The Peace.
The Silence.
With only the subtle splashing
of the waves
against the hull
of a sailboat.
The brilliant light
reflecting off of the Sea
into a fluorescent pool.
The stars twinkling;
Trying to compete
with the shimmering
Light of the moon.

There is no Beauty
like the expanse
of the Horizon at Sea.
It has the limits
of Landfall
with the illusion
of infinite sight.
Much like Man
who gives the illusion of
infinite Rationality --
but has the limits of Dreams.
It is those Dreams
that give Man the illusion
of Infinity --
without them,
Man would Perish.

There is no Beauty
like a Full Moon at Sea.
It is that Beauty
that gives Man
Dreams to pursue
and Rationality
to temporarily excuse.

The Heart of Sailing

Search deep
within your heart.
Will you find
that the beauty
of billowing sales
filled with gentle wind
are like the wings
of a dove –
soaring your spirit
into the clouds
beyond the earthly
World?

Or will you find
bitterness
that keeps you
entrenched in
the solid granite
of the cold shoreline –
where you spirit
Stagnates?

If,
deep within
your heart,
you find the wings
of a dove,
It doesn't matter
whether you soar
for a day,
for a month,
or for a year –
once you find
the love that enables you
to soar,
it is yours
Forever.

Seaside Sunrise

The cool mist of morning dew
is the first suggestion
that daylight approaches
as you wipe the sleep from your eyes
and awaken on the foredeck
of a gently rocking
sailboat.

As consciousness descends upon you,
you begin to see the beauty
that Nature has bestowed
on Mankind.

The scent of the salt air;
The sounds of the seagulls
as they seek their morning meal;
The vibrant turquoise of the Florida ocean;
And the colours that the rising sun
bestows on the few who are capable
of enveloping its
majesty.

Blanketing the ocean
are the brilliant hues of
yellow,
orange,
and red
that rise out the calm
turquoise
sea.

Those who have been graced with this sight
have been born to privilege;
with the depth,
the wisdom,
and the sensitivity
to appreciate
its true
beauty.

A Foggy Flight

The white of the sails
was barely visible
through the thick white blanket
that hovered mysteriously
around us.
The muffled clang
of the sea buoy
was the only indication
that land
could not be far
from the
security
of infinite space.

Our boat seemed to be
gliding gracefully -
alone -
through the chill
of the misty fog.
Suddenly,
everyone aboard
became as quiet
as the eerie
surroundings.

Unfamiliar voices
emerged from
the breathless silence.
Within the expanse
of the Pacific Ocean
we had found
a soul mate
from a boat
nearer than
than we imagined.

The mind
only gives the illusion of
Infinite Space.
but reality
brings us all
within
arms reach.

Life's Sail

The soul of sailing
consists of
unencumbered wind,
unwavering concentration
at the helm,
and creative sail trim.

Life provides each of us
with the same soul;
with the ability to see someone
who has the potential
to steal our unencumbered wind,
distract our unwavering concentration
at the helm of our world,
and rob us
of the ability to creatively
trim our sails
through life.

It is our choice,
as the Captain
of our own destiny,
to maintain the strength
and stamina
that controls the course
we choose to sail
and the ability
to sail that course
straight into the beauty
of the most spectacular
sunset.

The Sounds of Sailing

Peace
and Tranquility
are most often
the tender sounds
that are heard
while sailing
through the gentle breezes
created by
Mother Nature.

But when
Mother Nature's
gentle breezes
are supplanted by
mighty gusts of power,
Peace
and Tranquility
are transformed into a
wondrous symphony
inspired by
Her Fury.

The crashing of waves;
The rhythmic pounding of the sails;
the heightened pitch of voices
yearning to be hard
over the wind,
driving us with great
Command.

It is under these conditions
that Peace
and Tranquility
are quickly replaced with
Exhilaration and
Fear.
It is under these conditions
that we learn
true respect for
Mother Nature.

Summer Sailing

The summer sun
breathes fire
onto my bare
skin,
as the
light sea breezes
scarcely blow out
the flames.

The scent of
summer air
does not dry
the perspiration
from my skin;
it does not cool
my tender flesh.
Even the icy beer
barely soothes
my parched
throat.

But as
the occasional wave
splashes the salty spray
onto my face,
it is the beauty
of the sea,
and the sight
of the sails filled
with the light summer air,
that cool
the most important part of me –
my soul.

Images of Family

For My Mom

The joy of laughter;
the comfort of tears;
the peace of a warm smile;
These are the pleasures
I am limited
to receive
from you.

My love for you
runs through
my soul;
my compassion for you
soars through
my spirit.

May you
only accept
half of the love
I feel for you.
Then I would feel
true contentment.

For My Fabulous Mother

It is never the gift
that counts,
it is the sentiment
that has true
meaning.
Mine,
my dear mother,
is love and
friendship.
As we both age,
I find that Carolyn
was correct –
we cannot choose
our families.
You are more
than just family –
you are my friend.
I pick you
to be my mother
And more –
I pick you to be
my friend.
I guess I was just lucky.
I got both.

I wish I could be there
To spend your
special day with you
but my days
are special
because you
are a part
of my every day,
of my heart,
of my soul.

My Godmother

My godmother
is certainly
the female role model
by which I have fashioned
my feminine character.

There is no one
who has earned
any greater admiration,
respect,
or love
from me
than Auntie Renie.

She encompasses what every girl
should strive to exemplify
in terms of grace,
beauty,
and elegance -
and what every person
should strive to exemplify
in terms of rationality,
kindness,
honour,
and the ability to love.

She is a manifestation
of what is good
on this earth
and she will always
live in my
Heart.

Father of My Soul

Though our blood
does not run
through each other's veins,
nor are our genes
made in each other's image;
our spirits
have emerged
as One.

I have learned
the true meaning
of grace
and dignity
from He
who did not bear me;
I have learned
the true value
of the soul
from He
who did not
give me breath.

From He
I have been given
Life.
More important
`than breath,
it is the spirit
that has helped my essence
to soar.

These are the gifts
I have received
from you, Iwao.
The father of my soul.
Gifts I will treasure B
Always.

Happy 70th Birthday to my Father

Life may sometimes show its darker side,
but our love has surely proven
that depth of affection
emerges as a life force
that conquers all.

From you I have learned
the true meaning of love,
of selfless kindness,
and of strength of Spirit.

From you I have been given
the gift of life.
More important than breath,
the life you have given me
has allows my own spirit
to soar beyond the sky,
beyond the depths of the sea.
These are the gifts I have received
from you.
Gifts I will treasure - always.

On this, your 70th birthday,
I can only give you this,
the gift from my heart.

For my Late Tasha

(my gorgeous dog — Samoyed/Husky/Wolf mix)

From the tip of her
cold pink nose,
to the tip of her
fluffy white tail —
Tasha was filled
with love
and devotion.

From the tips of her
soft peach ears,
to the tips of her
tender white paws —
Tasha was filled
with merriment
and joy.

From the strangers
who briefly met her,
to my friends
who yearned to be near her,
to myself
who cherished her deeply —
Tasha will be missed
and loved
forever.

About the Author

Leslie E. Stern was born in Los Angeles, California, an only child. She graduated from the University of Miami in Coral Gables at twenty years old. She pursued her doctoral degree in philosophy and was offered an Assistant Professorship. She attained her Master's Degree in English literature. She went on to an illustrious career in public relations, garnering many prestigious clients but she never forgot her roots in fiction writing.

She wrote her first short story and her first poem when she was ten years old and has never stopped writing. Her passion comes from her family. Her step-father was world-renowned animation genius Iwao Takamoto, whom her mother married when Leslie was five years old. His passion for his own craft was such that he always boasted that he never worked a day in his life. When she is writing, it is not work. It is sheer pleasure as it has been since her childhood. Her mother continues to be a loving, supportive part of her life.

She is a published author and is currently completing the homage to her step-father "Living with a Legend", a non-fiction book of personal anecdotes about famous Iwao Takamoto.

Find out more about Leslie at:
www.leslieestern.com

www.ingramcontent.com/pod-product-compliance
Lightning Source LLC
Chambersburg PA
CBHW060459080526
44584CB00015B/1485